One Year of
Gratitude Journaling

A 52 week daily guide to cultivating a grateful,
positive attitude and attracting abundance.

Nicole Lockhart

SPECIAL BONUS!
Want this Bonus Book free?

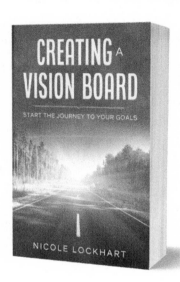

Get **FREE**, unlimited access to it and all of my new books by joining the Fan Base!

SCAN WITH YOUR CAMERA TO JOIN!

This Journal belongs to:

_____

Year:

_____

Gratitude

Cultivating an attitude of gratitude has been proven for thousands of years to bring inner joy, peace and prosperity to one's life. It also brings joy and peace to those around you. "Gratitude" has a Latin origin meaning "thankful" and "pleasing". It is one of life's great secrets that many people are rediscovering today.

grat•i•tude
\ ˈgra-tə-ˌtüd , -ˌtyüd \

: the quality of being thankful; readiness to show appreciation for and to return kindness.

It is no coincidence that gratitude and grace start with the same three letters, both come from the same word origin. When we adopt an attitude of gratitude, we are living in grace.

grace
\ ˈgrās \

: unmerited divine assistance given to humans for their regeneration or sanctification
: a state of sanctification enjoyed through divine assistance

When you are living life this way, everything will just seem to work out for you. Trust that the Universe will put you where you belong and help you along your life's journey to reach your goals and dreams.

So let's get started living your best possible life!

Week 1

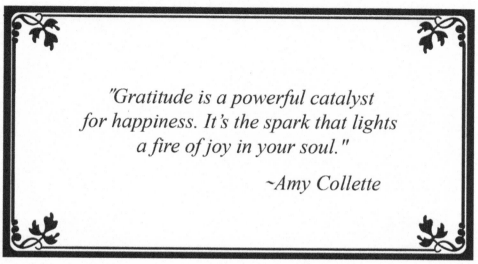

"Gratitude is a powerful catalyst for happiness. It's the spark that lights a fire of joy in your soul."

~Amy Collette

Today, I am grateful for: Date:

1)_____

2)_____

3)_____

Today, I am grateful for: Date:

1)_____

2)_____

3)_____

Today, I am grateful for: Date:

1)_____

2)_____

3)_____

Today, I am grateful for: _____ Date: _____

1)_____
2)_____
3)_____

Today, I am grateful for: _____ Date: _____

1)_____
2)_____
3)_____

Today, I am grateful for: _____ Date: _____

1)_____
2)_____
3)_____

Today, I am grateful for: _____ Date: _____

1)_____
2)_____
3)_____

This week:

Who made me smile?_____
Who inspired me?_____
What is the best thing that happened?_____
_____
What do I want to attract more of?_____
_____

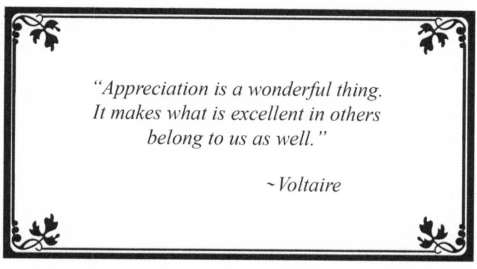

*"Appreciation is a wonderful thing.
It makes what is excellent in others
belong to us as well."*

~ Voltaire

Today, I am grateful for: Date:
1)_____
2)_____
3)_____

Today, I am grateful for: Date:
1)_____
2)_____
3)_____

Today, I am grateful for: Date:
1)_____
2)_____
3)_____

Today, I am grateful for: Date:

1)_____
2)_____
3)_____

Today, I am grateful for: Date:

1)_____
2)_____
3)_____

Today, I am grateful for: Date:

1)_____
2)_____
3)_____

Today, I am grateful for: Date:

1)_____
2)_____
3)_____

This week:

Who made me smile?_____
Who inspired me?_____
What is the best thing that happened?_____
_____
What do I want to attract more of?_____
_____

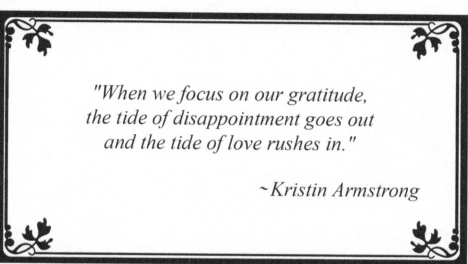

*"When we focus on our gratitude,
the tide of disappointment goes out
and the tide of love rushes in."*

~Kristin Armstrong

Today, I am grateful for: Date:
1)
2)
3)

Today, I am grateful for: Date:
1)
2)
3)

Today, I am grateful for: Date:
1)
2)
3)

Today, I am grateful for: Date:

1)_____

2)_____

3)_____

Today, I am grateful for: Date:

1)_____

2)_____

3)_____

Today, I am grateful for: Date:

1)_____

2)_____

3)_____

Today, I am grateful for: Date:

1)_____

2)_____

3)_____

This week:

Who made me smile?_____

Who inspired me?_____

What is the best thing that happened?_____

_____

What do I want to attract more of?_____

_____

Week 4

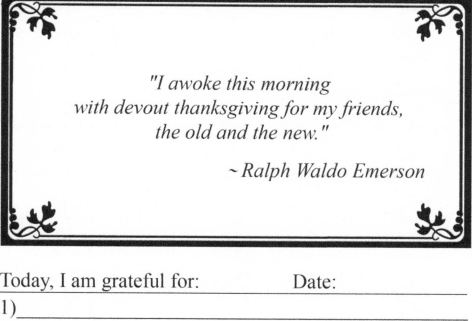

*"I awoke this morning
with devout thanksgiving for my friends,
the old and the new."*

~ Ralph Waldo Emerson

Today, I am grateful for: Date:

1)_____

2)_____

3)_____

Today, I am grateful for: Date:

1)_____

2)_____

3)_____

Today, I am grateful for: Date:

1)_____

2)_____

3)_____

Today, I am grateful for: Date:

1)_____
2)_____
3)_____

Today, I am grateful for: Date:

1)_____
2)_____
3)_____

Today, I am grateful for: Date:

1)_____
2)_____
3)_____

Today, I am grateful for: Date:

1)_____
2)_____
3)_____

This week:

Who made me smile?_____
Who inspired me?_____
What is the best thing that happened?_____
_____
What do I want to attract more of?_____
_____

Week 5

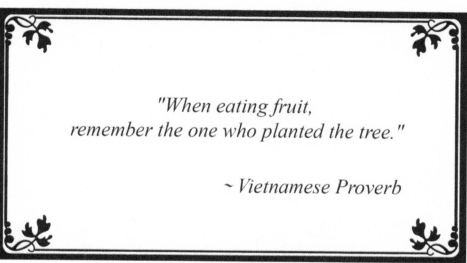

"When eating fruit,
remember the one who planted the tree."

~ Vietnamese Proverb

Today, I am grateful for: _____ Date: _____
1)_____
2)_____
3)_____

Today, I am grateful for: _____ Date: _____
1)_____
2)_____
3)_____

Today, I am grateful for: _____ Date: _____
1)_____
2)_____
3)_____

Today, I am grateful for: Date:

1)_____
2)_____
3)_____

Today, I am grateful for: Date:

1)_____
2)_____
3)_____

Today, I am grateful for: Date:

1)_____
2)_____
3)_____

Today, I am grateful for: Date:

1)_____
2)_____
3)_____

This week:

Who made me smile?_____
Who inspired me?_____
What is the best thing that happened?_____
_____
What do I want to attract more of?_____
_____

Week 6

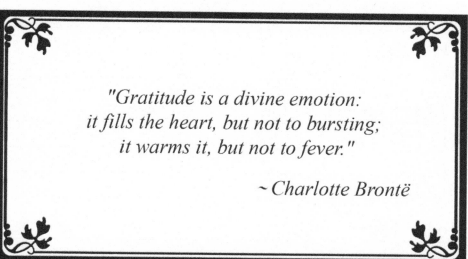

*"Gratitude is a divine emotion:
it fills the heart, but not to bursting;
it warms it, but not to fever."*

~ Charlotte Brontë

Today, I am grateful for: Date:
1)_____
2)_____
3)_____

Today, I am grateful for: Date:
1)_____
2)_____
3)_____

Today, I am grateful for: Date:
1)_____
2)_____
3)_____

Today, I am grateful for: _____ Date: _____

1)_____

2)_____

3)_____

Today, I am grateful for: _____ Date: _____

1)_____

2)_____

3)_____

Today, I am grateful for: _____ Date: _____

1)_____

2)_____

3)_____

Today, I am grateful for: _____ Date: _____

1)_____

2)_____

3)_____

This week:

Who made me smile?_____

Who inspired me?_____

What is the best thing that happened?_____

_____

What do I want to attract more of? _____

_____

Week 7

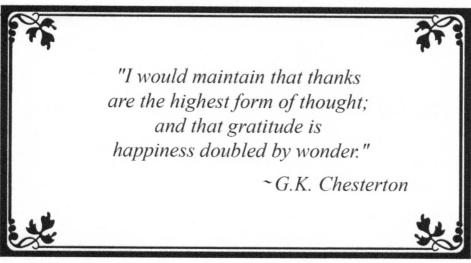

"I would maintain that thanks are the highest form of thought; and that gratitude is happiness doubled by wonder."

~G.K. Chesterton

Today, I am grateful for: Date:

1)_____

2)_____

3)_____

Today, I am grateful for: Date:

1)_____

2)_____

3)_____

Today, I am grateful for: Date:

1)_____

2)_____

3)_____

Today, I am grateful for: Date:
1)_____
2)_____
3)_____

Today, I am grateful for: Date:
1)_____
2)_____
3)_____

Today, I am grateful for: Date:
1)_____
2)_____
3)_____

Today, I am grateful for: Date:
1)_____
2)_____
3)_____

This week:

Who made me smile?_____
Who inspired me?_____
What is the best thing that happened?_____
_____
What do I want to attract more of?_____
_____

Week 8

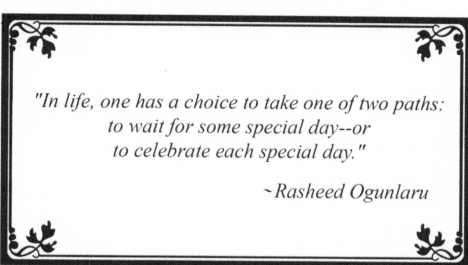

"In life, one has a choice to take one of two paths:
to wait for some special day--or
to celebrate each special day."

~Rasheed Ogunlaru

Today, I am grateful for: Date:
1)_____
2)_____
3)_____

Today, I am grateful for: Date:
1)_____
2)_____
3)_____

Today, I am grateful for: Date:
1)_____
2)_____
3)_____

Today, I am grateful for: Date:

1)_____
2)_____
3)_____

Today, I am grateful for: Date:

1)_____
2)_____
3)_____

Today, I am grateful for: Date:

1)_____
2)_____
3)_____

Today, I am grateful for: Date:

1)_____
2)_____
3)_____

This week:

Who made me smile?_____
Who inspired me?_____
What is the best thing that happened?_____
_____
What do I want to attract more of?_____
_____

Week 9

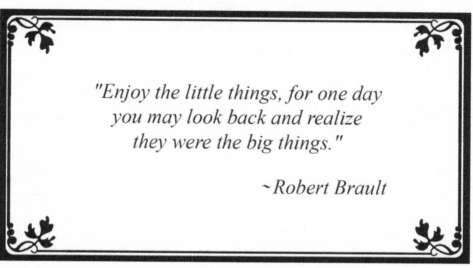

"Enjoy the little things, for one day you may look back and realize they were the big things."

~Robert Brault

Today, I am grateful for: Date: _____

1) _____

2) _____

3) _____

Today, I am grateful for: Date: _____

1) _____

2) _____

3) _____

Today, I am grateful for: Date: _____

1) _____

2) _____

3) _____

Today, I am grateful for: _____ Date: _____

1)_____
2)_____
3)_____

Today, I am grateful for: _____ Date: _____

1)_____
2)_____
3)_____

Today, I am grateful for: _____ Date: _____

1)_____
2)_____
3)_____

Today, I am grateful for: _____ Date: _____

1)_____
2)_____
3)_____

This week:

Who made me smile?_____
Who inspired me?_____
What is the best thing that happened?_____
_____
What do I want to attract more of?_____
_____

Week 10

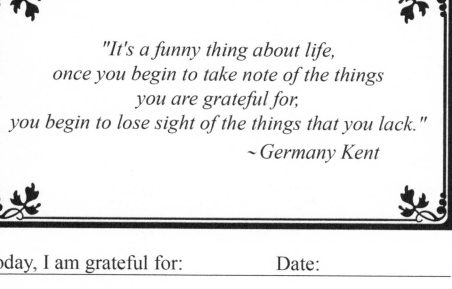

*"It's a funny thing about life,
once you begin to take note of the things
you are grateful for,
you begin to lose sight of the things that you lack."*
~ Germany Kent

Today, I am grateful for: Date:
1)_____
2)_____
3)_____

Today, I am grateful for: Date:
1)_____
2)_____
3)_____

Today, I am grateful for: Date:
1)_____
2)_____
3)_____

Today, I am grateful for: Date:

1)_____

2)_____

3)_____

Today, I am grateful for: Date:

1)_____

2)_____

3)_____

Today, I am grateful for: Date:

1)_____

2)_____

3)_____

Today, I am grateful for: Date:

1)_____

2)_____

3)_____

This week:

Who made me smile?_____

Who inspired me?_____

What is the best thing that happened?_____

_____

What do I want to attract more of?_____

_____

Week 11

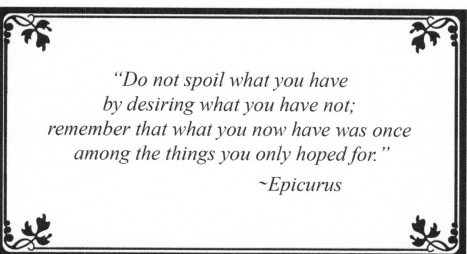

*"Do not spoil what you have
by desiring what you have not;
remember that what you now have was once
among the things you only hoped for."*

~Epicurus

Today, I am grateful for: Date: _____

1)_____

2)_____

3)_____

Today, I am grateful for: Date: _____

1)_____

2)_____

3)_____

Today, I am grateful for: Date: _____

1)_____

2)_____

3)_____

Today, I am grateful for: _____ Date: _____
1)_____
2)_____
3)_____

Today, I am grateful for: _____ Date: _____
1)_____
2)_____
3)_____

Today, I am grateful for: _____ Date: _____
1)_____
2)_____
3)_____

Today, I am grateful for: _____ Date: _____
1)_____
2)_____
3)_____

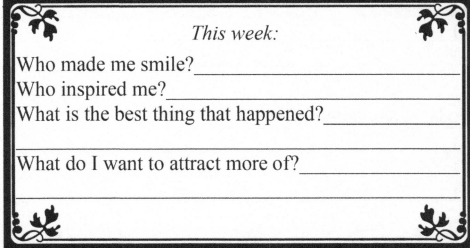

This week:

Who made me smile?_____
Who inspired me?_____
What is the best thing that happened?_____
_____
What do I want to attract more of?_____
_____

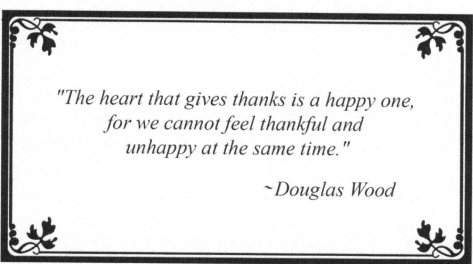

*"The heart that gives thanks is a happy one,
for we cannot feel thankful and
unhappy at the same time."*

~Douglas Wood

Today, I am grateful for: Date:

1)

2)

3)

Today, I am grateful for: Date:

1)

2)

3)

Today, I am grateful for: Date:

1)

2)

3)

Today, I am grateful for: Date:_____

1)_____

2)_____

3)_____

Today, I am grateful for: Date:_____

1)_____

2)_____

3)_____

Today, I am grateful for: Date:_____

1)_____

2)_____

3)_____

Today, I am grateful for: Date:_____

1)_____

2)_____

3)_____

This week:

Who made me smile?_____

Who inspired me?_____

What is the best thing that happened?_____

_____

What do I want to attract more of?_____

_____

> *"Piglet noticed that even though he had a*
> *Very Small Heart,*
> *it could hold a rather large amount of Gratitude."*
>
> *~A.A. Milne, 'Winnie-the-Pooh'*

Today, I am grateful for:　　　　Date: _____

1)_____

2)_____

3)_____

Today, I am grateful for:　　　　Date: _____

1)_____

2)_____

3)_____

Today, I am grateful for:　　　　Date: _____

1)_____

2)_____

3)_____

Today, I am grateful for: Date:

1)_____
2)_____
3)_____

Today, I am grateful for: Date:

1)_____
2)_____
3)_____

Today, I am grateful for: Date:

1)_____
2)_____
3)_____

Today, I am grateful for: Date:

1)_____
2)_____
3)_____

This week:

Who made me smile?_____
Who inspired me?_____
What is the best thing that happened?_____
_____
What do I want to attract more of?_____
_____

Week 14

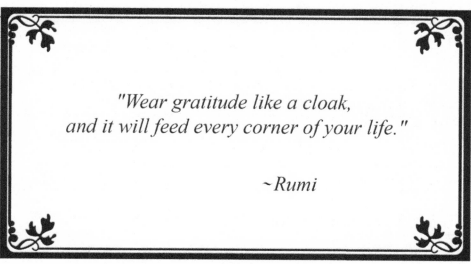

*"Wear gratitude like a cloak,
and it will feed every corner of your life."*

~Rumi

Today, I am grateful for: Date: _____
1)_____
2)_____
3)_____

Today, I am grateful for: Date: _____
1)_____
2)_____
3)_____

Today, I am grateful for: Date: _____
1)_____
2)_____
3)_____

Today, I am grateful for: Date:

1)_____

2)_____

3)_____

Today, I am grateful for: Date:

1)_____

2)_____

3)_____

Today, I am grateful for: Date:

1)_____

2)_____

3)_____

Today, I am grateful for: Date:

1)_____

2)_____

3)_____

This week:

Who made me smile?_____

Who inspired me?_____

What is the best thing that happened?_____

_____

What do I want to attract more of?_____

_____

Week 15

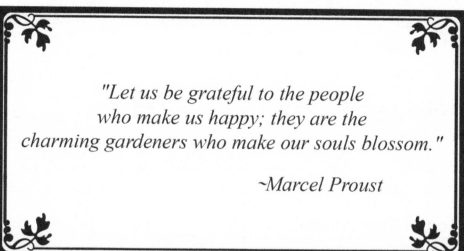

"Let us be grateful to the people who make us happy; they are the charming gardeners who make our souls blossom."

~Marcel Proust

Today, I am grateful for: Date:
1)_____
2)_____
3)_____

Today, I am grateful for: Date:
1)_____
2)_____
3)_____

Today, I am grateful for: Date:
1)_____
2)_____
3)_____

Today, I am grateful for: _____ Date: _____
1)_____
2)_____
3)_____

Today, I am grateful for: _____ Date: _____
1)_____
2)_____
3)_____

Today, I am grateful for: _____ Date: _____
1)_____
2)_____
3)_____

Today, I am grateful for: _____ Date: _____
1)_____
2)_____
3)_____

This week:

Who made me smile?_____
Who inspired me?_____
What is the best thing that happened?_____
_____
What do I want to attract more of?_____
_____

Week 16

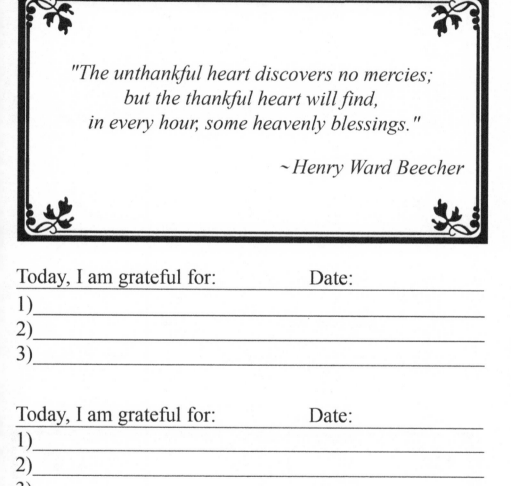

"The unthankful heart discovers no mercies; but the thankful heart will find, in every hour, some heavenly blessings."

~ Henry Ward Beecher

Today, I am grateful for: Date: _____

1)_____

2)_____

3)_____

Today, I am grateful for: Date: _____

1)_____

2)_____

3)_____

Today, I am grateful for: Date: _____

1)_____

2)_____

3)_____

Today, I am grateful for: Date:
1)_____
2)_____
3)_____

Today, I am grateful for: Date:
1)_____
2)_____
3)_____

Today, I am grateful for: Date:
1)_____
2)_____
3)_____

Today, I am grateful for: Date:
1)_____
2)_____
3)_____

This week:

Who made me smile?_____
Who inspired me?_____
What is the best thing that happened?_____
_____
What do I want to attract more of?_____
_____

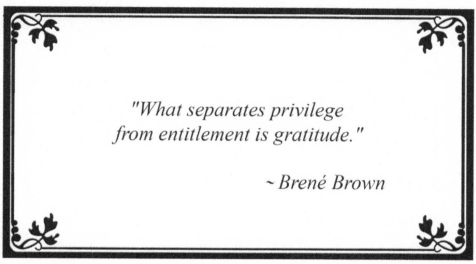

*"What separates privilege
from entitlement is gratitude."*

~ *Brené Brown*

Today, I am grateful for: Date:_____

1)_____

2)_____

3)_____

Today, I am grateful for: Date:_____

1)_____

2)_____

3)_____

Today, I am grateful for: Date:_____

1)_____

2)_____

3)_____

Today, I am grateful for: Date:_____
1)_____
2)_____
3)_____

Today, I am grateful for: Date:_____
1)_____
2)_____
3)_____

Today, I am grateful for: Date:_____
1)_____
2)_____
3)_____

Today, I am grateful for: Date:_____
1)_____
2)_____
3)_____

This week:

Who made me smile?_____
Who inspired me?_____
What is the best thing that happened?_____
_____
What do I want to attract more of?_____
_____

Week 18

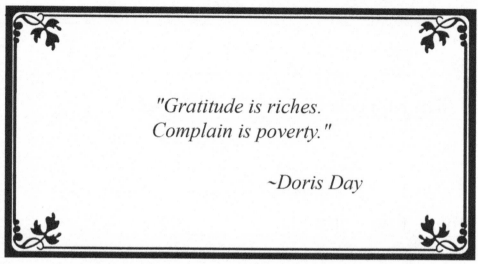

"Gratitude is riches.
Complain is poverty."

~Doris Day

Today, I am grateful for: Date:
1)_____
2)_____
3)_____

Today, I am grateful for: Date:
1)_____
2)_____
3)_____

Today, I am grateful for: Date:
1)_____
2)_____
3)_____

Today, I am grateful for: Date:
1)_____
2)_____
3)_____

Today, I am grateful for: Date:
1)_____
2)_____
3)_____

Today, I am grateful for: Date:
1)_____
2)_____
3)_____

Today, I am grateful for: Date:
1)_____
2)_____
3)_____

This week:

Who made me smile?_____
Who inspired me?_____
What is the best thing that happened?_____
_____
What do I want to attract more of?_____
_____

Week 19

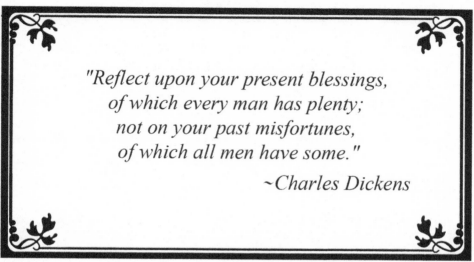

"Reflect upon your present blessings,
of which every man has plenty;
not on your past misfortunes,
of which all men have some."

~Charles Dickens

Today, I am grateful for: Date:
1)
2)
3)

Today, I am grateful for: Date:
1)
2)
3)

Today, I am grateful for: Date:
1)
2)
3)

Today, I am grateful for: Date:_____
1)_____
2)_____
3)_____

Today, I am grateful for: Date:_____
1)_____
2)_____
3)_____

Today, I am grateful for: Date:_____
1)_____
2)_____
3)_____

Today, I am grateful for: Date:_____
1)_____
2)_____
3)_____

This week:

Who made me smile?_____
Who inspired me?_____
What is the best thing that happened?_____
_____
What do I want to attract more of?_____
_____

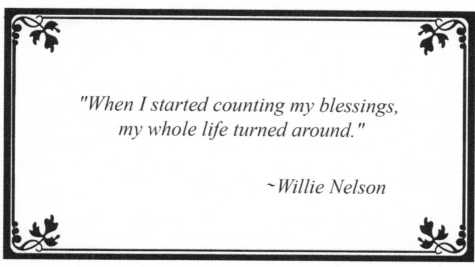

*"When I started counting my blessings,
my whole life turned around."*

~Willie Nelson

Today, I am grateful for: Date:
1)_____
2)_____
3)_____

Today, I am grateful for: Date:
1)_____
2)_____
3)_____

Today, I am grateful for: Date:
1)_____
2)_____
3)_____

Today, I am grateful for: Date:

1)_____
2)_____
3)_____

Today, I am grateful for: Date:

1)_____
2)_____
3)_____

Today, I am grateful for: Date:

1)_____
2)_____
3)_____

Today, I am grateful for: Date:

1)_____
2)_____
3)_____

This week:

Who made me smile?_____
Who inspired me?_____
What is the best thing that happened?_____
_____
What do I want to attract more of?_____
_____

Week 21

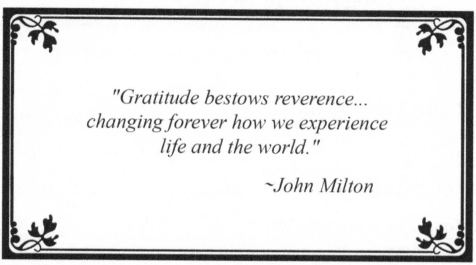

*"Gratitude bestows reverence...
changing forever how we experience
life and the world."*

~John Milton

Today, I am grateful for: Date: _____
1) _____
2) _____
3) _____

Today, I am grateful for: Date: _____
1) _____
2) _____
3) _____

Today, I am grateful for: Date: _____
1) _____
2) _____
3) _____

Today, I am grateful for: Date:
1)_____
2)_____
3)_____

Today, I am grateful for: Date:
1)_____
2)_____
3)_____

Today, I am grateful for: Date:
1)_____
2)_____
3)_____

Today, I am grateful for: Date:
1)_____
2)_____
3)_____

This week:

Who made me smile?_____
Who inspired me?_____
What is the best thing that happened?_____
_____
What do I want to attract more of?_____
_____

Week 22

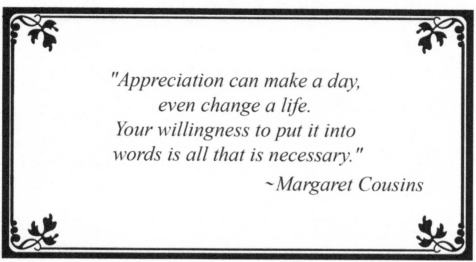

*"Appreciation can make a day,
even change a life.
Your willingness to put it into
words is all that is necessary."*

~Margaret Cousins

Today, I am grateful for: Date:

1)_____

2)_____

3)_____

Today, I am grateful for: Date:

1)_____

2)_____

3)_____

Today, I am grateful for: Date:

1)_____

2)_____

3)_____

Today, I am grateful for: Date:

1)_____

2)_____

3)_____

Today, I am grateful for: Date:

1)_____

2)_____

3)_____

Today, I am grateful for: Date:

1)_____

2)_____

3)_____

Today, I am grateful for: Date:

1)_____

2)_____

3)_____

This week:

Who made me smile?_____

Who inspired me?_____

What is the best thing that happened?_____

_____

What do I want to attract more of?_____

_____

Week 23

"Forget yesterday - it has already forgotten you.
Don't sweat tomorrow - you haven't even met.
Instead, open your eyes and your
heart to a truly precious gift - today."

~Steve Maraboli

Today, I am grateful for: Date:

1)_____

2)_____

3)_____

Today, I am grateful for: Date:

1)_____

2)_____

3)_____

Today, I am grateful for: Date:

1)_____

2)_____

3)_____

Today, I am grateful for: Date:
1)_____
2)_____
3)_____

Today, I am grateful for: Date:
1)_____
2)_____
3)_____

Today, I am grateful for: Date:
1)_____
2)_____
3)_____

Today, I am grateful for: Date:
1)_____
2)_____
3)_____

This week:

Who made me smile?_____
Who inspired me?_____
What is the best thing that happened?_____
_____
What do I want to attract more of?_____
_____

Week 24

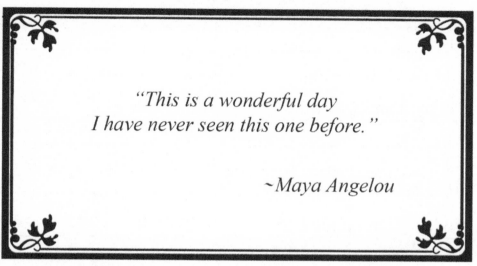

"This is a wonderful day
I have never seen this one before."

~Maya Angelou

Today, I am grateful for: Date: _____

1)_____

2)_____

3)_____

Today, I am grateful for: Date: _____

1)_____

2)_____

3)_____

Today, I am grateful for: Date: _____

1)_____

2)_____

3)_____

Today, I am grateful for:_____ Date:_____
1)_____
2)_____
3)_____

Today, I am grateful for:_____ Date:_____
1)_____
2)_____
3)_____

Today, I am grateful for:_____ Date:_____
1)_____
2)_____
3)_____

Today, I am grateful for:_____ Date:_____
1)_____
2)_____
3)_____

This week:

Who made me smile?_____
Who inspired me?_____
What is the best thing that happened?_____
_____
What do I want to attract more of?_____
_____

Week 25

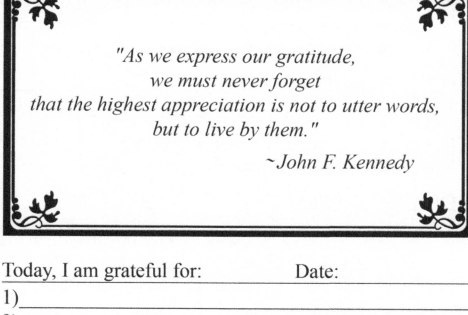

*"As we express our gratitude,
we must never forget
that the highest appreciation is not to utter words,
but to live by them."*

~John F. Kennedy

Today, I am grateful for: Date: _____

1)_____

2)_____

3)_____

Today, I am grateful for: Date: _____

1)_____

2)_____

3)_____

Today, I am grateful for: Date: _____

1)_____

2)_____

3)_____

Today, I am grateful for: Date:

1)_____
2)_____
3)_____

Today, I am grateful for: Date:

1)_____
2)_____
3)_____

Today, I am grateful for: Date:

1)_____
2)_____
3)_____

Today, I am grateful for: Date:

1)_____
2)_____
3)_____

This week:

Who made me smile?_____
Who inspired me?_____
What is the best thing that happened?_____
_____
What do I want to attract more of?_____
_____

Week 26

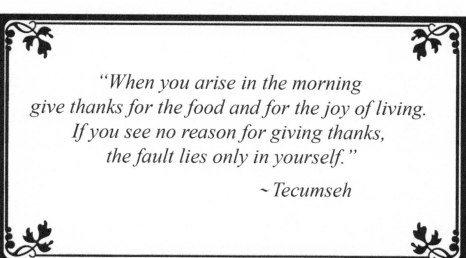

"When you arise in the morning
give thanks for the food and for the joy of living.
If you see no reason for giving thanks,
the fault lies only in yourself."

~ Tecumseh

Today, I am grateful for: Date:
1)_____
2)_____
3)_____

Today, I am grateful for: Date:
1)_____
2)_____
3)_____

Today, I am grateful for: Date:
1)_____
2)_____
3)_____

Today, I am grateful for: Date:_____

1)_____
2)_____
3)_____

Today, I am grateful for: Date:_____

1)_____
2)_____
3)_____

Today, I am grateful for: Date:_____

1)_____
2)_____
3)_____

Today, I am grateful for: Date:_____

1)_____
2)_____
3)_____

This week:

Who made me smile?_____
Who inspired me?_____
What is the best thing that happened?_____
_____
What do I want to attract more of?_____
_____

Week 27

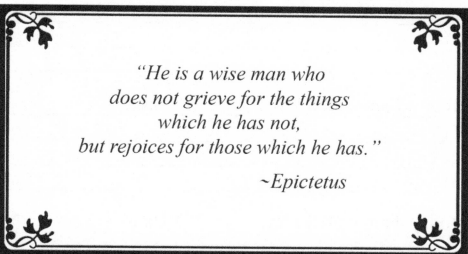

*"He is a wise man who
does not grieve for the things
which he has not,
but rejoices for those which he has."*

~Epictetus

Today, I am grateful for: Date:
1)
2)
3)

Today, I am grateful for: Date:
1)
2)
3)

Today, I am grateful for: Date:
1)
2)
3)

Today, I am grateful for: Date:

1)_____

2)_____

3)_____

Today, I am grateful for: Date:

1)_____

2)_____

3)_____

Today, I am grateful for: Date:

1)_____

2)_____

3)_____

Today, I am grateful for: Date:

1)_____

2)_____

3)_____

This week:

Who made me smile?_____

Who inspired me?_____

What is the best thing that happened?_____

_____

What do I want to attract more of?_____

_____

Week 28

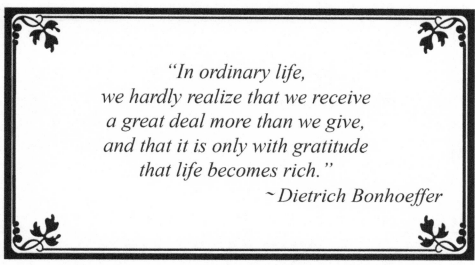

*"In ordinary life,
we hardly realize that we receive
a great deal more than we give,
and that it is only with gratitude
that life becomes rich."*
~ *Dietrich Bonhoeffer*

Today, I am grateful for: Date: _____
1)_____
2)_____
3)_____

Today, I am grateful for: Date: _____
1)_____
2)_____
3)_____

Today, I am grateful for: Date: _____
1)_____
2)_____
3)_____

Today, I am grateful for: Date:

1)_____
2)_____
3)_____

Today, I am grateful for: Date:

1)_____
2)_____
3)_____

Today, I am grateful for: Date:

1)_____
2)_____
3)_____

Today, I am grateful for: Date:

1)_____
2)_____
3)_____

This week:

Who made me smile?_____
Who inspired me?_____
What is the best thing that happened?_____
_____
What do I want to attract more of?_____
_____

Week 29

*"Cultivate the habit of being grateful
for every good thing that comes to you,
and to give thanks continuously. And because all things
have contributed to your advancement,
you should include all things in your gratitude."*

~ Ralph Waldo Emerson

Today, I am grateful for: _____ Date: _____

1)_____

2)_____

3)_____

Today, I am grateful for: _____ Date: _____

1)_____

2)_____

3)_____

Today, I am grateful for: _____ Date: _____

1)_____

2)_____

3)_____

Today, I am grateful for: Date:

1)_____
2)_____
3)_____

Today, I am grateful for: Date:

1)_____
2)_____
3)_____

Today, I am grateful for: Date:

1)_____
2)_____
3)_____

Today, I am grateful for: Date:

1)_____
2)_____
3)_____

This week:

Who made me smile?_____
Who inspired me?_____
What is the best thing that happened?_____
_____
What do I want to attract more of?_____
_____

Week 30

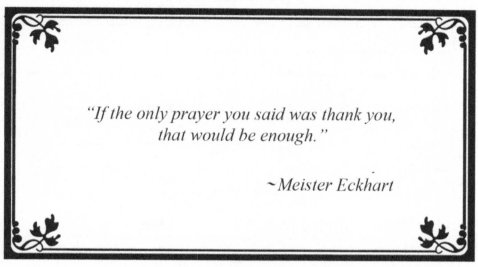

"If the only prayer you said was thank you, that would be enough."

~Meister Eckhart

Today, I am grateful for: Date:
1)_____
2)_____
3)_____

Today, I am grateful for: Date:
1)_____
2)_____
3)_____

Today, I am grateful for: Date:
1)_____
2)_____
3)_____

Today, I am grateful for: Date: _____

1)_____

2)_____

3)_____

Today, I am grateful for: Date: _____

1)_____

2)_____

3)_____

Today, I am grateful for: Date: _____

1)_____

2)_____

3)_____

Today, I am grateful for: Date: _____

1)_____

2)_____

3)_____

This week:

Who made me smile?_____

Who inspired me?_____

What is the best thing that happened?_____

_____

What do I want to attract more of?_____

_____

Week 31

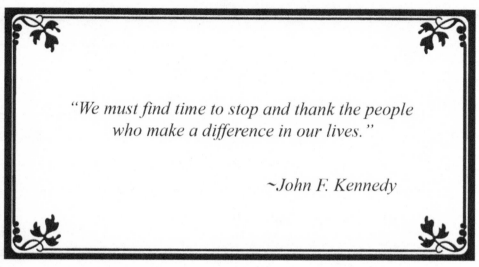

"We must find time to stop and thank the people who make a difference in our lives."

~John F. Kennedy

Today, I am grateful for: _____ Date: _____
1)_____
2)_____
3)_____

Today, I am grateful for: _____ Date: _____
1)_____
2)_____
3)_____

Today, I am grateful for: _____ Date: _____
1)_____
2)_____
3)_____

Today, I am grateful for: Date:

1)_____
2)_____
3)_____

Today, I am grateful for: Date:

1)_____
2)_____
3)_____

Today, I am grateful for: Date:

1)_____
2)_____
3)_____

Today, I am grateful for: Date:

1)_____
2)_____
3)_____

This week:

Who made me smile?_____
Who inspired me?_____
What is the best thing that happened?_____
_____
What do I want to attract more of?_____
_____

Week 32

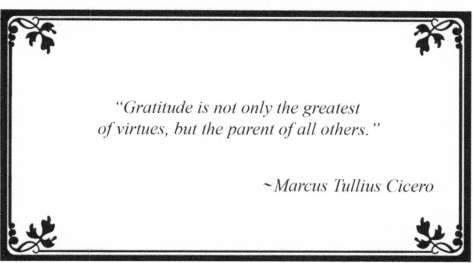

*"Gratitude is not only the greatest
of virtues, but the parent of all others."*

~Marcus Tullius Cicero

Today, I am grateful for: Date: _____

1)_____

2)_____

3)_____

Today, I am grateful for: Date: _____

1)_____

2)_____

3)_____

Today, I am grateful for: Date: _____

1)_____

2)_____

3)_____

Today, I am grateful for:　　　　　　Date:_____

1)_____
2)_____
3)_____

Today, I am grateful for:　　　　　　Date:_____

1)_____
2)_____
3)_____

Today, I am grateful for:　　　　　　Date:_____

1)_____
2)_____
3)_____

Today, I am grateful for:　　　　　　Date:_____

1)_____
2)_____
3)_____

This week:

Who made me smile?_____
Who inspired me?_____
What is the best thing that happened?_____
_____
What do I want to attract more of?_____
_____

Week 33

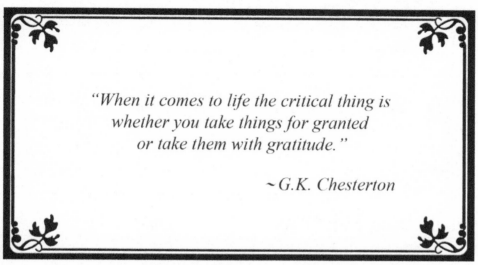

*"When it comes to life the critical thing is
whether you take things for granted
or take them with gratitude."*

~ *G.K. Chesterton*

Today, I am grateful for: Date:
1)_____
2)_____
3)_____

Today, I am grateful for: Date:
1)_____
2)_____
3)_____

Today, I am grateful for: Date:
1)_____
2)_____
3)_____

Today, I am grateful for: Date:_____

1)_____
2)_____
3)_____

Today, I am grateful for: Date:_____

1)_____
2)_____
3)_____

Today, I am grateful for: Date:_____

1)_____
2)_____
3)_____

Today, I am grateful for: Date:_____

1)_____
2)_____
3)_____

This week:

Who made me smile?_____
Who inspired me?_____
What is the best thing that happened?_____
_____
What do I want to attract more of?_____
_____

Week 34

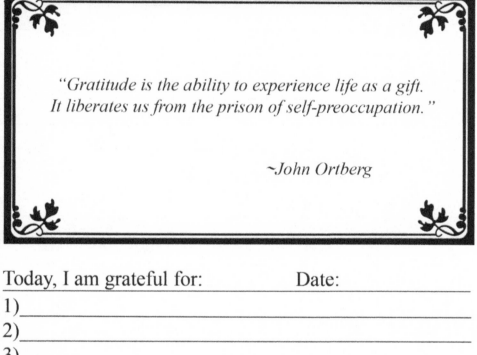

*"Gratitude is the ability to experience life as a gift.
It liberates us from the prison of self-preoccupation."*

~John Ortberg

Today, I am grateful for: Date:

1)_____

2)_____

3)_____

Today, I am grateful for: Date:

1)_____

2)_____

3)_____

Today, I am grateful for: Date:

1)_____

2)_____

3)_____

Today, I am grateful for: Date:

1)_____
2)_____
3)_____

Today, I am grateful for: Date:

1)_____
2)_____
3)_____

Today, I am grateful for: Date:

1)_____
2)_____
3)_____

Today, I am grateful for: Date:

1)_____
2)_____
3)_____

This week:

Who made me smile?_____
Who inspired me?_____
What is the best thing that happened?_____
_____
What do I want to attract more of?_____
_____

Week 35

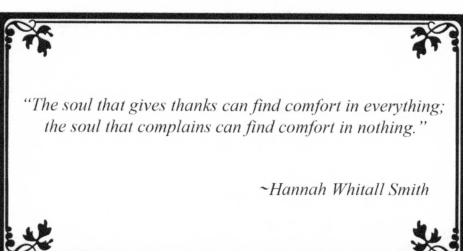

"The soul that gives thanks can find comfort in everything; the soul that complains can find comfort in nothing."

~Hannah Whitall Smith

Today, I am grateful for: Date: _____
1)_____
2)_____
3)_____

Today, I am grateful for: Date: _____
1)_____
2)_____
3)_____

Today, I am grateful for: Date: _____
1)_____
2)_____
3)_____

Today, I am grateful for: Date:

1)_____
2)_____
3)_____

Today, I am grateful for: Date:

1)_____
2)_____
3)_____

Today, I am grateful for: Date:

1)_____
2)_____
3)_____

Today, I am grateful for: Date:

1)_____
2)_____
3)_____

This week:

Who made me smile?_____
Who inspired me?_____
What is the best thing that happened?_____
_____
What do I want to attract more of?_____
_____

Week 36

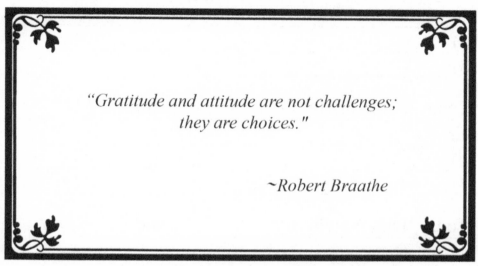

"Gratitude and attitude are not challenges; they are choices."

~Robert Braathe

Today, I am grateful for: _____ Date: _____
1)_____
2)_____
3)_____

Today, I am grateful for: _____ Date: _____
1)_____
2)_____
3)_____

Today, I am grateful for: _____ Date: _____
1)_____
2)_____
3)_____

Today, I am grateful for: Date:
1)_____
2)_____
3)_____

Today, I am grateful for: Date:
1)_____
2)_____
3)_____

Today, I am grateful for: Date:
1)_____
2)_____
3)_____

Today, I am grateful for: Date:
1)_____
2)_____
3)_____

This week:

Who made me smile?_____
Who inspired me?_____
What is the best thing that happened?_____
_____
What do I want to attract more of?_____
_____

Week 37

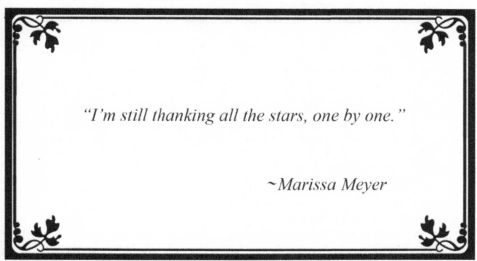

"I'm still thanking all the stars, one by one."

~Marissa Meyer

Today, I am grateful for: Date:

1)_____

2)_____

3)_____

Today, I am grateful for: Date:

1)_____

2)_____

3)_____

Today, I am grateful for: Date:

1)_____

2)_____

3)_____

Today, I am grateful for:　　　　Date:

1)_____
2)_____
3)_____

Today, I am grateful for:　　　　Date:

1)_____
2)_____
3)_____

Today, I am grateful for:　　　　Date:

1)_____
2)_____
3)_____

Today, I am grateful for:　　　　Date:

1)_____
2)_____
3)_____

This week:

Who made me smile?_____
Who inspired me?_____
What is the best thing that happened?_____
_____
What do I want to attract more of?_____
_____

Week 38

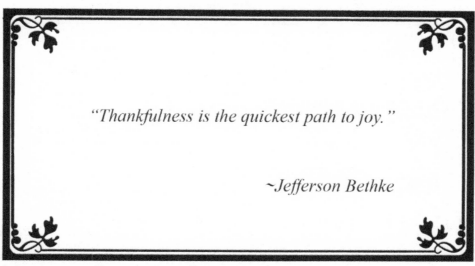

"Thankfulness is the quickest path to joy."

~Jefferson Bethke

Today, I am grateful for: Date: _____
1)_____
2)_____
3)_____

Today, I am grateful for: Date: _____
1)_____
2)_____
3)_____

Today, I am grateful for: Date: _____
1)_____
2)_____
3)_____

Today, I am grateful for: Date:
1)_____
2)_____
3)_____

Today, I am grateful for: Date:
1)_____
2)_____
3)_____

Today, I am grateful for: Date:
1)_____
2)_____
3)_____

Today, I am grateful for: Date:
1)_____
2)_____
3)_____

This week:

Who made me smile?_____
Who inspired me?_____
What is the best thing that happened?_____
_____
What do I want to attract more of?_____
_____

Week 39

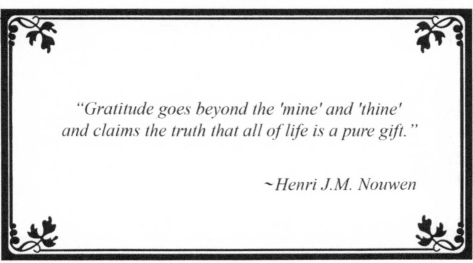

*"Gratitude goes beyond the 'mine' and 'thine'
and claims the truth that all of life is a pure gift."*

~Henri J.M. Nouwen

Today, I am grateful for: Date: _____
1)_____
2)_____
3)_____

Today, I am grateful for: Date: _____
1)_____
2)_____
3)_____

Today, I am grateful for: Date: _____
1)_____
2)_____
3)_____

Today, I am grateful for: Date:_____

1)_____
2)_____
3)_____

Today, I am grateful for: Date:_____

1)_____
2)_____
3)_____

Today, I am grateful for: Date:_____

1)_____
2)_____
3)_____

Today, I am grateful for: Date:_____

1)_____
2)_____
3)_____

This week:

Who made me smile?_____
Who inspired me?_____
What is the best thing that happened?_____
_____
What do I want to attract more of?_____
_____

Week 40

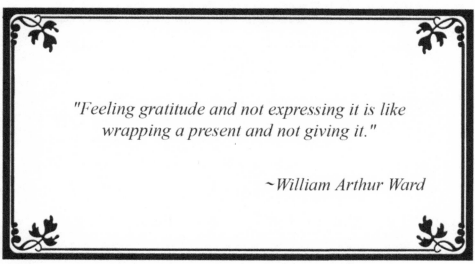

"Feeling gratitude and not expressing it is like wrapping a present and not giving it."

~William Arthur Ward

Today, I am grateful for: Date:
1)_____
2)_____
3)_____

Today, I am grateful for: Date:
1)_____
2)_____
3)_____

Today, I am grateful for: Date:
1)_____
2)_____
3)_____

Today, I am grateful for: Date:

1)_____
2)_____
3)_____

Today, I am grateful for: Date:

1)_____
2)_____
3)_____

Today, I am grateful for: Date:

1)_____
2)_____
3)_____

Today, I am grateful for: Date:

1)_____
2)_____
3)_____

This week:

Who made me smile?_____
Who inspired me?_____
What is the best thing that happened?_____
_____
What do I want to attract more of?_____
_____

Week 41

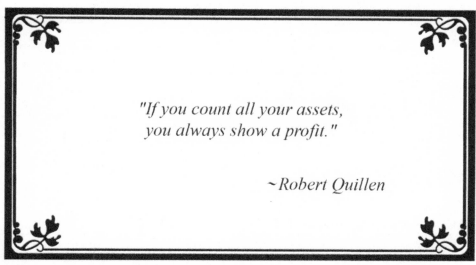

*"If you count all your assets,
you always show a profit."*

~Robert Quillen

Today, I am grateful for: Date: _____

1) _____

2) _____

3) _____

Today, I am grateful for: Date: _____

1) _____

2) _____

3) _____

Today, I am grateful for: Date: _____

1) _____

2) _____

3) _____

Today, I am grateful for: Date:

1)_____
2)_____
3)_____

Today, I am grateful for: Date:

1)_____
2)_____
3)_____

Today, I am grateful for: Date:

1)_____
2)_____
3)_____

Today, I am grateful for: Date:

1)_____
2)_____
3)_____

This week:

Who made me smile?_____
Who inspired me?_____
What is the best thing that happened?_____
_____
What do I want to attract more of?_____
_____

Week 42

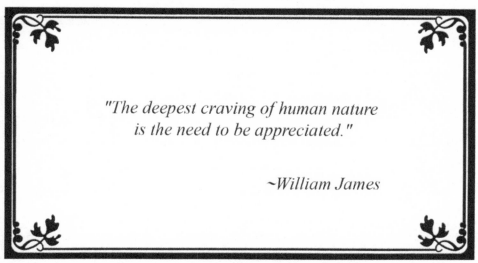

*"The deepest craving of human nature
is the need to be appreciated."*

~William James

Today, I am grateful for: Date:
1)_____
2)_____
3)_____

Today, I am grateful for: Date:
1)_____
2)_____
3)_____

Today, I am grateful for: Date:
1)_____
2)_____
3)_____

Today, I am grateful for: _____ Date: _____
1)_____
2)_____
3)_____

Today, I am grateful for: _____ Date: _____
1)_____
2)_____
3)_____

Today, I am grateful for: _____ Date: _____
1)_____
2)_____
3)_____

Today, I am grateful for: _____ Date: _____
1)_____
2)_____
3)_____

This week:

Who made me smile?_____
Who inspired me?_____
What is the best thing that happened?_____
_____
What do I want to attract more of?_____
_____

Week 43

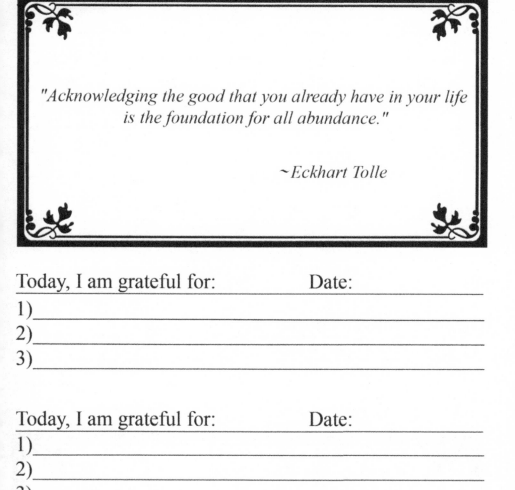

"Acknowledging the good that you already have in your life is the foundation for all abundance."

~Eckhart Tolle

Today, I am grateful for: Date:
1)_____
2)_____
3)_____

Today, I am grateful for: Date:
1)_____
2)_____
3)_____

Today, I am grateful for: Date:
1)_____
2)_____
3)_____

Today, I am grateful for: Date:_____

1)_____

2)_____

3)_____

Today, I am grateful for: Date:_____

1)_____

2)_____

3)_____

Today, I am grateful for: Date:_____

1)_____

2)_____

3)_____

Today, I am grateful for: Date:_____

1)_____

2)_____

3)_____

This week:

Who made me smile?_____

Who inspired me?_____

What is the best thing that happened?_____

_____

What do I want to attract more of?_____

_____

Week 44

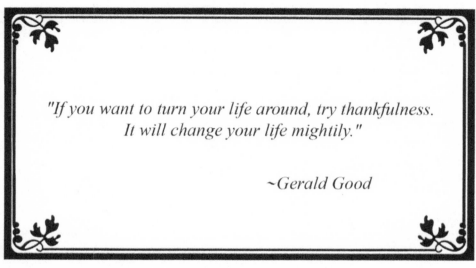

"If you want to turn your life around, try thankfulness. It will change your life mightily."

~Gerald Good

Today, I am grateful for: Date:_____
1)_____
2)_____
3)_____

Today, I am grateful for: Date:_____
1)_____
2)_____
3)_____

Today, I am grateful for: Date:_____
1)_____
2)_____
3)_____

Today, I am grateful for: Date:_____
1)_____
2)_____
3)_____

Today, I am grateful for: Date:_____
1)_____
2)_____
3)_____

Today, I am grateful for: Date:_____
1)_____
2)_____
3)_____

Today, I am grateful for: Date:_____
1)_____
2)_____
3)_____

This week:

Who made me smile?_____
Who inspired me?_____
What is the best thing that happened?_____
_____
What do I want to attract more of?_____
_____

"The world has enough beautiful mountains and meadows, spectacular skies and serene lakes. It has enough lush forests, flowered fields, and sandy beaches. It has plenty of stars and the promise of a new sunrise and sunset every day. What the world needs more of is people to appreciate and enjoy it."

~Michael Josephson

Today, I am grateful for: Date:
1)_____
2)_____
3)_____

Today, I am grateful for: Date:
1)_____
2)_____
3)_____

Today, I am grateful for: Date:
1)_____
2)_____
3)_____

Today, I am grateful for: Date:

1)_____

2)_____

3)_____

Today, I am grateful for: Date:

1)_____

2)_____

3)_____

Today, I am grateful for: Date:

1)_____

2)_____

3)_____

Today, I am grateful for: Date:

1)_____

2)_____

3)_____

This week:

Who made me smile?_____

Who inspired me?_____

What is the best thing that happened?_____

_____

What do I want to attract more of?_____

_____

Week 46

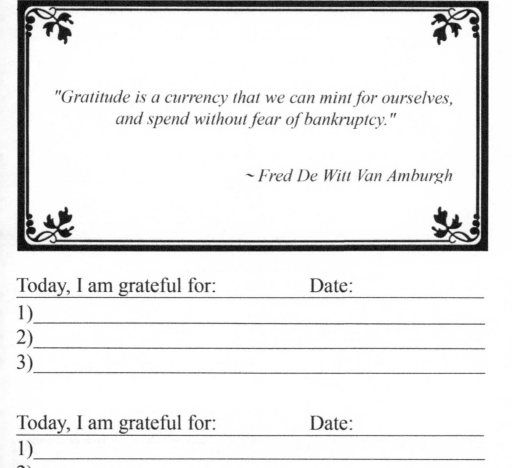

"Gratitude is a currency that we can mint for ourselves, and spend without fear of bankruptcy."

~ Fred De Witt Van Amburgh

Today, I am grateful for: Date: _____

1) _____

2) _____

3) _____

Today, I am grateful for: Date: _____

1) _____

2) _____

3) _____

Today, I am grateful for: Date: _____

1) _____

2) _____

3) _____

Today, I am grateful for: Date:

1)_____
2)_____
3)_____

Today, I am grateful for: Date:

1)_____
2)_____
3)_____

Today, I am grateful for: Date:

1)_____
2)_____
3)_____

Today, I am grateful for: Date:

1)_____
2)_____
3)_____

This week:

Who made me smile?_____
Who inspired me?_____
What is the best thing that happened?_____
_____
What do I want to attract more of?_____
_____

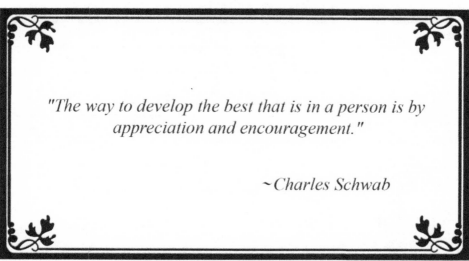

"The way to develop the best that is in a person is by appreciation and encouragement."

~Charles Schwab

Today, I am grateful for: Date:
1)_____
2)_____
3)_____

Today, I am grateful for: Date:
1)_____
2)_____
3)_____

Today, I am grateful for: Date:
1)_____
2)_____
3)_____

Today, I am grateful for: Date:_____

1)_____
2)_____
3)_____

Today, I am grateful for: Date:_____

1)_____
2)_____
3)_____

Today, I am grateful for: Date:_____

1)_____
2)_____
3)_____

Today, I am grateful for: Date:_____

1)_____
2)_____
3)_____

This week:

Who made me smile?_____
Who inspired me?_____
What is the best thing that happened?_____
_____
What do I want to attract more of?_____
_____

Week 48

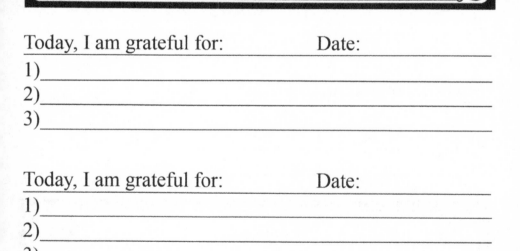

*"At times, our own light goes out
and is rekindled by a spark from another person.
Each of us has cause to think with deep gratitude of those
who have lighted the flame within us."*

~Albert Schweitzer

Today, I am grateful for: Date:_____

1)_____

2)_____

3)_____

Today, I am grateful for: Date:_____

1)_____

2)_____

3)_____

Today, I am grateful for: Date:_____

1)_____

2)_____

3)_____

Today, I am grateful for: Date:

1)_____
2)_____
3)_____

Today, I am grateful for: Date:

1)_____
2)_____
3)_____

Today, I am grateful for: Date:

1)_____
2)_____
3)_____

Today, I am grateful for: Date:

1)_____
2)_____
3)_____

This week:

Who made me smile?_____
Who inspired me?_____
What is the best thing that happened?_____
_____
What do I want to attract more of?_____
_____

Week 49

"Let us rise up and be thankful, for if we didn't learn a lot today, at least we learned a little, and if we didn't learn a little, at least we didn't get sick, and if we got sick, at least we didn't die; so, let us all be thankful."

~ Buddha

Today, I am grateful for: Date: _____

1) _____
2) _____
3) _____

Today, I am grateful for: Date: _____

1) _____
2) _____
3) _____

Today, I am grateful for: Date: _____

1) _____
2) _____
3) _____

Today, I am grateful for: Date: _____

1)_____

2)_____

3)_____

Today, I am grateful for: Date: _____

1)_____

2)_____

3)_____

Today, I am grateful for: Date: _____

1)_____

2)_____

3)_____

Today, I am grateful for: Date: _____

1)_____

2)_____

3)_____

This week:

Who made me smile?_____

Who inspired me?_____

What is the best thing that happened?_____

_____

What do I want to attract more of?_____

_____

Week 50

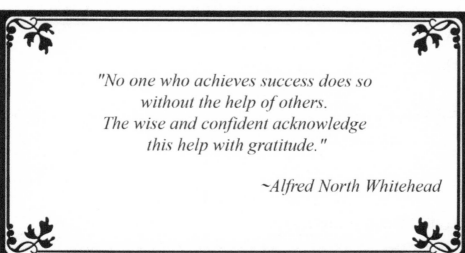

"No one who achieves success does so without the help of others. The wise and confident acknowledge this help with gratitude."

~Alfred North Whitehead

Today, I am grateful for: Date:

1)_____

2)_____

3)_____

Today, I am grateful for: Date:

1)_____

2)_____

3)_____

Today, I am grateful for: Date:

1)_____

2)_____

3)_____

Today, I am grateful for: Date:_____

1)_____
2)_____
3)_____

Today, I am grateful for: Date:_____

1)_____
2)_____
3)_____

Today, I am grateful for: Date:_____

1)_____
2)_____
3)_____

Today, I am grateful for: Date:_____

1)_____
2)_____
3)_____

This week:

Who made me smile?_____
Who inspired me?_____
What is the best thing that happened?_____
_____
What do I want to attract more of?_____
_____

Week 51

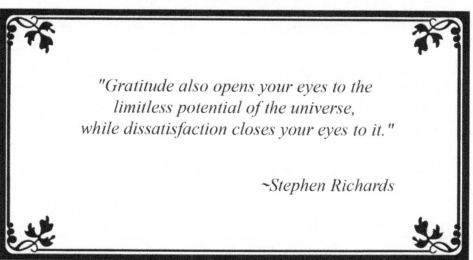

"Gratitude also opens your eyes to the limitless potential of the universe, while dissatisfaction closes your eyes to it."

~Stephen Richards

Today, I am grateful for: Date:_____
1)_____
2)_____
3)_____

Today, I am grateful for: Date:_____
1)_____
2)_____
3)_____

Today, I am grateful for: Date:_____
1)_____
2)_____
3)_____

Today, I am grateful for: Date: _____

1)_____

2)_____

3)_____

Today, I am grateful for: Date: _____

1)_____

2)_____

3)_____

Today, I am grateful for: Date: _____

1)_____

2)_____

3)_____

Today, I am grateful for: Date: _____

1)_____

2)_____

3)_____

This week:

Who made me smile?_____

Who inspired me?_____

What is the best thing that happened?_____

_____

What do I want to attract more of?_____

_____

Week 52

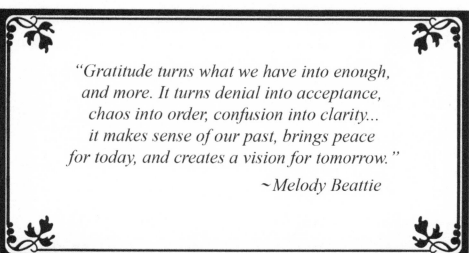

"Gratitude turns what we have into enough,
and more. It turns denial into acceptance,
chaos into order, confusion into clarity...
it makes sense of our past, brings peace
for today, and creates a vision for tomorrow."

~Melody Beattie

Today, I am grateful for: Date:

1)_____

2)_____

3)_____

Today, I am grateful for: Date:

1)_____

2)_____

3)_____

Today, I am grateful for: Date:

1)_____

2)_____

3)_____

Today, I am grateful for: Date:_____
1)_____
2)_____
3)_____

Today, I am grateful for: Date:_____
1)_____
2)_____
3)_____

Today, I am grateful for: Date:_____
1)_____
2)_____
3)_____

Today, I am grateful for: Date:_____
1)_____
2)_____
3)_____

This week:

Who made me smile?_____
Who inspired me?_____
What is the best thing that happened?_____
_____
What do I want to attract more of?_____
_____

Congratulations on finishing
One Year of Gratitude Journaling!

I hope your life has been enriched and that
you continue to practice gratitude daily so that
you can live your best possible life!

Made in United States
Orlando, FL
08 December 2022

25914433R00071